BECOMING A *Ballerina*

A *NUTCRACKER* STORY, starring the dancers of Boston Ballet

Lise Friedman & Mary Dowdle

VIKING
An Imprint of Penguin Group (USA) Inc.

VIKING

Published by the Penguin Group

Penguin Young Readers Group, 345 Hudson Street, New York, New York 10014, U.S.A.

Penguin Group (Canada), 90 Eglinton Avenue East, Suite 700, Toronto, Ontario,

Canada M4P 2Y3 (a division of Pearson Penguin Canada Inc.)

Penguin Books Ltd, 80 Strand, London WC2R 0RL, England

Penguin Ireland, 25 St Stephen's Green, Dublin 2, Ireland (a division of Penguin Books Ltd)

Penguin Group (Australia), 250 Camberwell Road, Camberwell, Victoria 3124,

Australia (a division of Pearson Australia Group Pty Ltd)

Penguin Books India Pvt Ltd, 11 Community Centre, Panchsheel Park, New Delhi–110 017, India

Penguin Group (NZ), 67 Apollo Drive, Rosedale, Auckland 0632,

New Zealand (a division of Pearson New Zealand Ltd.)

Penguin Books (South Africa) (Pty) Ltd, 24 Sturdee Avenue, Rosebank, Johannesburg 2196, South Africa

Penguin Books Ltd, Registered Offices: 80 Strand, London WC2R 0RL, England

First published in the United States of America by Viking, a division of Penguin Young Readers Group, 2012

10 9 8 7 6 5 4 3 2 1

Text copyright © Lise Friedman, 2012

Photographs copyright © Mary Dowdle, 2012

All rights reserved

LIBRARY OF CONGRESS CATALOGING-IN-PUBLICATION DATA

Friedman, Lise.

Becoming a ballerina : a nutcracker story / by Lise Friedman ; photographs by Mary Dowdle.

p. cm.

ISBN 978-0-670-01392-0 (hardcover)

1. Ballet dancing—Juvenile literature. 2. Ballerinas—Juvenile literature. I. Dowdle, Mary, ill. II. Title.

GV1787.5.F74 2012   792.8—dc23   2012000867

Manufactured in China   Set in Requiem Text   Book design by Kate Renner

ALWAYS LEARNING   PEARSON

For aspiring dancers and their devoted families,
with special thanks to our own families for their unwavering support

ACKNOWLEDGMENTS

Realizing *Becoming a Ballerina* required the efforts of many people. Thank you to all. To Margaux, Jacqueline, and Colin, for inspiring the idea behind the book; Fiona, her mother, Noriko, and her sisters, Bronwyn and Delia, for their unflagging interest and active participation; Mikko Nissinen, Mariel MacNaughton (our invaluable liaison), Margaret Tracey, Leslie Cargill, Melanie Atkins, Jennifer Markham, Christopher Hird, Sabi Varga, Audrey Reny, and all of the dancers, teachers, staff, students, and crew at Boston Ballet and Boston Opera House, for inviting us into your classrooms, rehearsal studios, and backstage to witness the preparation and production of Boston Ballet's *The Nutcracker*; Leila Sales, our editor, art director Denise Cronin, Kate Renner, *Becoming a Ballerina*'s designer, and everyone at Viking Children's Books, for your enthusiasm, support, and guidance; and our agent, Jennifer Unter.

"*Half hour!*" the stage manager calls.

"Oh, no!" I say, rummaging through the accessories box. "I can't find Clara's necklace!"

"Here you are, Fiona," the wardrobe supervisor says soothingly. "It was in the compartment marked 'Clara's necklace.'"

"Oh, right," I say. "Whoops." I put on the necklace. It's hard not to be a little panicky tonight. We're half an hour away from the opening night performance of Boston Ballet's *Nutcracker*, and I'm playing Clara, the girl who is given the magical nutcracker.

"Let's get your back buttoned up properly." The wardrobe supervisor turns me around.

"This dress is so heavy," I tell her. "I feel like I'm wearing a big satin curtain. It pulls me off balance, especially in pirouettes. But I like how it's all princess-y and old-fashioned. Why can't we dress like this today?"

"Good question. Please hold still."

While I'm holding still, Farin bounces over to me. Farin is one of my best friends at Boston Ballet School. We like to do splits together. Sometimes we challenge ourselves by balancing between two chairs and seeing if we can stretch our legs more than 180 degrees.

"I feel like my muscles are ice cold," I whisper to her.

"That's ridiculous," she replies, adjusting her sash. "You've been warming up nonstop since six o'clock."

"That's not exactly true." Then I explain to Farin what I've actually been doing since I signed in. First I stretched and talked to everybody for about forty-five minutes. Then I went to the makeup and wig area along with Max (the dancer who plays Clara's little brother, Fritz) and the Party Boys. There are *never* enough boys in ballet, so the girls who play boys in the party scene have to wear boy wigs. I'm glad that's not me.

Max and I are the only kids who have to get our makeup done by the makeup artist—except for the lambs, who get their noses painted. In general, Boston Ballet wants kids to look like kids, but since Fritz and Clara are onstage so much, the audience needs to see their features clearly. With all the lights, dancers need makeup to outline their eyes and define their mouths.

Stage makeup is not your average street makeup. "It's scary to see my face up close," I say to Farin, turning to glance at myself in the mirror. "I look like a completely different person. It makes me feel glamorous.

"Anyway," I go on, as the wardrobe supervisor finishes buttoning my dress, "no matter how much I warm up, I'll never be as flexible as Misa!"

"It's like she doesn't have any bones," Farin agrees.

We both watch principal dancer Misa Kuranaga across the room. She's dancing the role of the Sugar Plum Fairy tonight, which is the most famous and difficult role in *The Nutcracker*. Right now she's warming up at the barre, arching her back so far that her head is practically touching the floor.

"Hi girls." She waves from upside down. "Have a wonderful show!"

I look around at the other company dancers. They're not like Farin and me, chattering away. Some of the adult dancers are stretching in their warm-up suits. Others are practicing steps or just marking with their feet while moving their arms fully. They sip water, talk softly, and listen to their iPods. They're all business and don't look nervous. I, on the other hand, am fighting serious butterflies, even though I've been averaging ten hours of rehearsal a week since October.

"Okay, Lambs, upstairs!" calls Jennifer Markham, one of our teachers. "Careful, Reindeer, with those antlers." She's bringing the Soldiers, Mice, and Reindeer kids in to wardrobe. The wardrobe area would be too crowded if all

the *Nutcracker* children were here at once, so after they get dressed, kids wait in the second-floor dressing rooms until right before they need to get ready to go onstage. The Soldiers are used to lining up, but some of the littlest kids who play the Mice are all over the place, bumping headpieces and swatting each other with their tails.

"Fifteen minutes!"

I know that some dancers get upset if they can't concentrate undisturbed until the last minute, but I just want to go over my steps once and spend the rest of the time with my friends—talking, singing songs, and doing our special handshake. I kind of made up the handshake during rehearsals, but all my friends added parts to it—like ways of saying "good luck" in different languages. I taught them the Japanese equivalent, which is *"ganbatte."*

"Oodgay ucklay!" says Farin in her best Pig Latin.

"Five minutes!"

Max and I and the Party Kids who aren't in the prologue go to stage left, behind the party scenery. There we wait, listening to the grand, romantic-sounding overture. Meanwhile, the backstage crew is moving sets, pulling curtains, organizing props. My heart is beating in my throat.

"Places!"

This is it.

The rest of the Party Kids go onstage and prepare for their frozen-in-time moment, while Max and I wait with the dancer who plays our Governess. I hum along to the music and try to

put myself in my Clara Silberhaus frame of mind: a young girl living in a small town in Germany in 1835 who's excited for Christmas, who adores her friends and family, and who sometimes even likes her annoying little brother.

But my twenty-first-century Bostonian self keeps interrupting. *What if I fall? Or forget a step? Can I land that double* tour en l'air? *My entire family is out there tonight, and loads of my school friends.*

In rehearsal a few weeks ago, Mikko Nissinen, Boston Ballet's artistic director and the choreographer of *The Nutcracker*, told us, "The ballet is the story of Clara growing up." The audience has to see her change because "she is the character they connect to the most. They see the ballet through her eyes."

That's me. That's what I have to do now.

Right before our cue, I take a deep breath to try to stop the fluttering in my stomach. I give Max a look that means *let's go*, and we rush onstage and into the lights.

This isn't just another rehearsal. This is the real deal.

The performance has begun. ⟶

Nutcracker auditions are Saturday and Sunday, September 25 and 26. Dancers are spread out everywhere, stretching. When we are called to line up, I go to the hallway outside Studio 7 with Farin, Alexandra, and a bunch of other girls from my ballet class. We all pin numbers to our leotards. I'm number 702.

"Alexandra, will you help me fix my bun?" I ask. Alexandra's buns are always really pretty and stay in place even when she pirouettes.

"Sure." She reaches up to try to help me. "Wow, Fiona, you put so much spray in your hair it feels like plastic."

Farin giggles.

"I just don't want it to get in my eyes!" I defend myself.

"Please come in," says Ms. Markham, opening the door to the studio.

Inside, I can feel the lights on my chest. The artistic staff is sitting in the front of the room at long tables. All our nervous chatting fades to silence in a flash. My legs are wobbling.

Melanie Atkins, the children's ballet mistress, walks to the center of the room and says, "Let's begin with the 'tea step.'"

It's terrifying trying to learn the step with the judges seeing everything we do. Their expressions never change as they whisper back and forth. Then we have to perform it: once starting on our left foot and once starting on our right. Since Farin and I are two of the smallest dancers at our level, we are the first to go. (We're eligible for roles based on our height and levels.)

"Thank you," Ms. Atkins says once we're done, and that's it. Five minutes at the most, and my fate is decided. Luckily, I've done well enough to get a red callback slip when I leave, which means another audition tomorrow morning.

There are eighty-seven roles for children in *The Nutcracker,* including the Party Children, Mice, Soldiers, Dolls, Cavalry, Shepherdesses, Tea Dancers, Lambs, Sugar Plum Fairy Attendants, and Polichinelles, the little French clowns who pop out from under Mother Ginger's giant skirt. And, of course, Clara and Fritz.

When I was nine, I asked a friend of my mom's if she thought I could be Clara one day. She said, "Actually, no, dear. There's so much competition for the part."

I was devastated. But as usual my mom came to the rescue. "We never know what we will be, Fiona. You just have to do your best and enjoy."

I hope my mom was right. And I hope her friend was wrong.

"MOM, I'M SO STRESSED." THE FIRST DAY OF auditions is over, and I can hardly eat my dinner.

"I know just how you, feel, Fiona," says my sixteen-year-old sister, Bronwyn.

"Me too!" pipes up nine-year-old Delia.

Bronwyn and Delia are also dancers at Boston Ballet School, and we all auditioned for this year's production of *The Nutcracker.* And we all got callback slips!

"I'm so proud of you, girls." My mom kisses the top of each of our heads. "The only things to

worry about now are resting, focusing, and looking forward to tomorrow."

At the Sunday callbacks, ten of us are taken from Studio 5, where we all wait, to Studio 7.

"Please come to the center of the room," says Ms. Atkins. She teaches us the "Clara step" in front of Mr. Nissinen and the rest of the artistic staff. My legs are almost as shaky as they were yesterday, but I manage to concentrate and don't forget any of the step.

"Thank you, girls," says Mr. Nissinen after we finish.

"How do you think you did?" Alexandra asks me as we walk downstairs. Now we have to wait until we're called back to Studio 7 with the rest of the kids to do steps from the party scene and tea dance.

"Not sure," I say. "I was nervous, but I think I did okay. You?"

"Me, too." She sighs. "I tried not to look at the artistic staff while I was dancing."

"Too scary!" agrees Farin. "And my bun was flopping up and down when I jumped."

Fifty-four kids were cut from the first round, so there are 306 of us at callbacks, trying for 247 parts in one of the three *Nutcracker* casts. I'm relieved that I made it this far, and I tell myself that I'll be happy to get any part at all, but what I really want, more than anything, is to be cast as Clara.

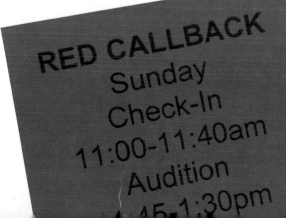

RED CALLBACK
Sunday
Check-In
11:00-11:40am
Audition
1:30pm

WHEN MY SISTERS AND I COME HOME FROM ballet class one week after callbacks, a casting letter is waiting for each of us.

Bronwyn opens hers first. "I got Shepherdess!"

"My turn." Delia tears open her envelope. "I got Black Lamb!" she screams.

"Great," laughs Bronwyn. "I get to shepherd you around the stage."

I pick up my envelope and slowly open the flap. I can hardly breathe. I read the letter and almost shriek, "I got the part! I'm Clara!"

"Fantastic!" shouts Bronwyn, grabbing me in a huge hug. "Look, the most important advice I can give you is to genuinely have fun onstage."

Bronwyn should know. She performed Clara two years in a row, when she was in seventh and eighth grade. "Everything won't go perfectly," she tells me. "But trust me, you'll be able to pull off

just about anything without the audience knowing whether you've flopped on purpose or not."

"Yeah, right, Miss Perfect. If I fall on my face everyone will think that I did it on purpose?"

"Seriously, in one of my performances as Clara, Uncle Drosselmeier and I had just stood up from our wooden throne in Act Two when Mother Ginger tripped on her dress and fell over."

"I remember," I interrupt. "I was actually trapped underneath Mother Ginger's skirt when that happened. Since we were onstage we had to be silent until the stagehands could let us out."

"Right! But Dross saved the show because he immediately started to improvise, so I did, too, and we made it through until the curtain could be lowered. If we could recover from that, you can recover from any mistake you might make as Clara!"

"Anyway," my mom adds, laughing, "I'm sure you won't fall on your face, Fiona."

"Hey, what about me?" Delia asks. She's upside down in one of her handstands. Delia has been at Boston Ballet School practically all her life, so everyone knows her. "Congratulate me!" she says.

"I'm very proud of you, Delia," my mom says, and tickles her toes.

"Being the Black Lamb is more fun than being any of the other Lambs," Delia says, flopping down onto her feet, "because I get to jump around a lot and I love jumping, and also because I get to do the opposite of everyone else. My

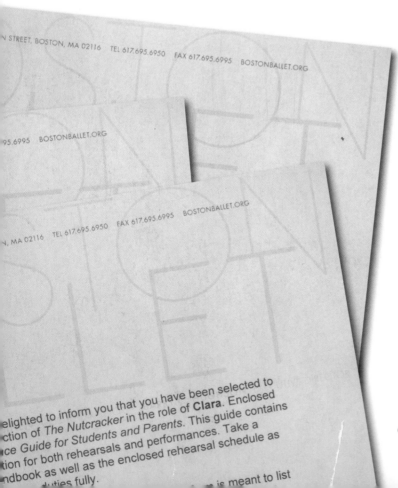

STREET, BOSTON, MA 02116   TEL 617.695.6950   FAX 617.695.6995   BOSTONBALLET.ORG

95.6995   BOSTONBALLET.ORG

MA 02116   TEL 617.695.6950   FAX 617.695.6995   BOSTONBALLET.ORG

N, MA 02116   TEL 617.695.6950   FAX 617.695.6995   BOSTONBALLET.ORG

elighted to inform you that you have been selected to ction of *The Nutcracker* in the role of **Clara**. Enclosed ce Guide for Students and Parents. This guide contains tion for both rehearsals and performances. Take a ndbook as well as the enclosed rehearsal schedule as duties fully.

is meant to list

character is the little lamb who does everything wrong."

While my little sister demonstrates her jumping skills, I read over my letter again. I still can't believe I'm going to play Clara, the most important child in *The Nutcracker*. I've performed in the ballet before, but this feels different.

When I was eight, I got the part of the Marzipan Doll. The next year I was the Gingerbread Man, and then a Mouse and a Polichinelle, and last year I was a Party Girl. This *Nutcracker* season, both of my sisters and I will be together onstage. I'm glad we're in the same cast. I'll get to watch Bronwyn shepherd Delia and the other Lambs during Act Two, when Clara sits on the throne with Uncle Drosselmeier.

Eventually my mom says, "Okay, girls, back to reality. Upstairs and get started on your home-

work." But I take my letter from the Boston Ballet with me and spend most of the evening practicing steps in front of the full-length mirror on our bathroom door. I wish rehearsals were starting this second. ⟶

"Let's start from the top of the party scene," Ms. Atkins says, clapping her hands. Ms. Atkins used to dance with the company, and she still does everything perfectly. She can stand on pointe in her tennis shoes.

When we perform the party scene at the opera house, the stage will be filled with company dancers, kids in fancy dresses, and a beautiful Christmas tree. But today the girls are just wearing rehearsal skirts, and Ms. Atkins has to play Uncle Drosselmeier because we don't start rehearsing with the company dancers for another three weeks.

"Pay close attention to the counts," Ms. Atkins says. "You two Party Boys, stop chit-chatting. That won't do when you rehearse with the company."

Suddenly, the music becomes intensely dramatic. We silently count 1-2-3-4-5-6-7-8, pretending the parents are dancing, then run "onstage." Uncle Drosselmeier makes "his" clumsy entrance after us. He's so excited to show off his nutcracker doll that he trips, and his gifts fly into the air and onto the floor.

Come here, Dross mimes to Fritz and Clara. Then he gives Clara the nutcracker doll.

Nobody speaks in the ballet, so the audience has to be able to piece together the story from our gestures. Having a script running through my head helps me to understand exactly what I'm miming.

Uncle Drosselmeier, I mime now, *he is absolutely beautiful. Did you make him yourself? May I hold him?*

I can have him? Thank you! Mama, Papa, Grandma, Grandpa, look what Uncle Drosselmeier gave me. I work on my *épaulement* as Clara does a little dance around the room to show everyone her nutcracker.

Once we've run through the scene a number of times, Ms. Atkins tells us to take a short break before running the Clara solo.

are seventy-seven from the first floor to Studio 7 at the very top. My mom jokes that this might be part of Boston Ballet's secret training to make their dancers even stronger.

My friends and I find a spot on the carpet to stretch and eat our lunch. Some of my friends didn't get parts in *The Nutcracker* this year, or didn't get the parts they wanted. I try not to talk

We grab our dance bags from the studio floor and head for the hallway. "Hey, Alexandra, want to trade sandwiches?" I reach into my bag for my peanut butter and jelly and grimace. "Ugh. My abs are killing me."

"I know!" Alexandra agrees, giving me half of her egg salad. "We're like a couple of old ladies. It even hurts to laugh."

I have to admit that on top of being sore from class, climbing all the stairs at the ballet school wipes me out. I counted them once, and there

too much about rehearsals around them when we see one another in class or in the hall. I know I shouldn't feel guilty for getting what I wanted, but sometimes I can't help it.

The little kids are bouncing around us while their moms try to get them to hold still long enough to put their hair up. I know what level each of the girls is by the color of her leotard. Light pink is for the very beginners, then it goes white, turquoise, light blue, candy pink (that's Delia), butter yellow, violet, sea green, burgundy (what I wore last year), liberty blue (what I wear now that I'm in Pre-professional II), black, hunter green (Bronwyn), and finally black cherry. After that, you're a pro.

When I was the age of those squirmy kids, in my light-blue leotard, I wasn't sure yet if ballet was really "my thing." "You know, Fiona," my mom said when I was about Delia's age, "just

Claras, "The only way the audience will believe you is if you believe you. You are overjoyed that Uncle Drosselmeier has given you the nutcracker. Fiona, will you start?"

I take the first few steps of Clara's solo.

"Fiona, you need to extend your right arm a bit more here, so we can see that you're really reaching."

because Bronwyn is dancing doesn't mean you have to follow her. You are two different people." So I tried lots of activities in addition to my dance classes. I fell in love with singing for a while. I also did figure skating and fencing and won some competitions. Then I realized ballet was what I cared about most.

Now I almost get knocked over by the little kids running into the studio. I throw away my sandwich bag and follow them inside. Break over.

Back in the studio, Ms. Atkins tells the

I'm reaching with a water bottle instead of the nutcracker because Ms. Atkins doesn't allow any actual nutcrackers in rehearsal until closer to opening night. "By then, we will be inundated with nutcrackers," she says.

"How are you getting into your last *arabesque?*" she asks me.

Ms. Atkins is trying to get us to put the movements together so they mean more than just steps, so they look like a mini-performance. Once I've finished the solo, she says, "Instead of just doing an *arabesque*, and then thinking, now I'm going for a *chassé*, your *arabesque* should lead you into your *chassé*, which naturally leaves your head behind and gives you that nice *épaulement effacé*, which opens your chest so the audience can see you. Work on that, Fiona. Alexandra, you're up next."

There are five of us learning the part of Clara: Isabelle, Alexandra, Chelsea, Farin, and me. I'm in Cast A and dance Clara in fourteen of the forty *Nutcrackers* this season. Alexandra is in Cast B, and Chelsea and Isabelle share Cast C. They're called "half Claras." They do half their performances as Clara and the other half as a Party Girl. Alexandra was a half Clara last year, so she's excited to have twice as many shows this time. Farin is the understudy.

Even though we're different ages and levels, and we go to different schools, the Claras get to know one another really well from all the time

we spend waiting and stretching in the lounges. Sometimes we talk about guys, or celebrities we like. Unfortunately, once the performances begin we'll be with our separate casts, so after that I won't get to hang out with the other Claras that much. The exception is Farin, who is a Party Girl in my cast in addition to being the Clara understudy. I hope she'll get at least one chance to dance the part of Clara onstage this season.

When I watch the other Claras, I can see how Ms. Atkins wants the solo to look. Each of us does something a little different with the choreography.

"Very nice arms," Ms. Atkins compliments Alexandra. "They're nicely curved so your *port de bras* doesn't look too sharp."

Alexandra's so graceful. Watching her makes me feel like I have to work on my ballet running. Ms. Atkins tells us to point our feet when running, but also to look more like a girl running to hug her mom and less like a ballerina.

I'm anxious about performing the section that comes after the solo, when Drosselmeier picks up Clara and spins her around really fast. Yesterday, before ballet class, I ran into Sabi Varga, one of the Drosselmeiers. "Hey, Fiona," he said, "let's give that spin a whirl." He swung me around quickly. When he put me down, I was so dizzy I landed on my butt next to the water fountain.

"I'm not going to swing you around, Fiona," Ms. Atkins says now. "Just run around me and imagine you're in the air."

That goes well, mostly since I don't have to leave the ground.

I'M MOST WORRIED ABOUT PERFORMING the moment in the battle scene when I have to throw my shoe so it hits the Mouse King.

"I'm not surprised you're having trouble with that," my mom says the next week, when she picks us up after school. "Bronwyn had the same problem when she was Clara." Today I have a little extra time between getting picked up by my mom, cramming in some homework, and rehearsal—All Battle and All Party, 5:00–8:30. I usually have to change into my dance clothes and do my hair in the backseat of the car.

My mom goes on, "I prayed for two years straight that Bronwyn would hit the Mouse King—anywhere. Once she threw the shoe way over his head and he had to pretend he got hit."

"Gee, Mom, thanks," groans Bronwyn.

"After we drop off your sisters at rehearsal, let's use the extra time to practice throwing a softball in our backyard."

My mom always helps me when I have trouble. She never complains about the hours she spends in the car every day, driving us back and forth from school to ballet to home. And on top of all that, she teaches piano.

"Okay, Fiona. Throw from the shoulder, not the wrist. Extend your arm."

While I try to throw the softball so it lands anywhere near my mother, I mostly think about school today and how much homework I have to get done after rehearsal tonight.

I have lots of good friends at the ballet school, but it's different with my regular school friends. I don't get to hang out after school or on weekends, because I'm always in class or rehearsal, so I just have to hope that we have the same lunch. I miss going to birthday parties and the movies, being in school talent shows, sleepovers—normal stuff.

Some of my classmates don't understand why

I dance so much. Today a boy in my math class asked, "Do you make a lot of money?"

"I don't get paid to dance," I explained. "But I get to be on a real stage with professional dancers, and I get lots of help and feedback from the artistic staff. And I get to go to a party when the season is over."

He made a face, like, *So?*

That's when Serena came to my rescue. Serena is one of my best school friends. She loves gymnastics as much as I love ballet, and sometimes we talk about body conditioning and healthy food. She plays the piano, like me.

"Maybe we can have a sleepover soon," Serena said. "When you're done with *Nutcracker*."

That's not going to be for another month and a half, but I said yes, anyway. "If you come to my house, just be ready for an early morning wake-up from you-know-who," I warned her.

"You-know-who" is Delia. She is a human alarm clock, which is probably her most annoying habit. Her second most annoying habit is that she's decided it is her job to keep track of Bronwyn's and my chores. She tells me to fold the laundry, and when it's time to start the rice.

We have rice almost every night, because my mom is from Japan. Before she came to America she directed opera companies in Osaka, Tokyo, and Kobe. My middle name, Amane, comes from a kanji character in my mom's name and means "good fortune around." Bronwyn's is Mako and means "pure, genuine, true child," and Delia's, Kotone, means "harp music."

My parents are divorced. They separated

when I was nine years old. My father was born in England. He's an infectious disease doctor. Last year he remarried, and I now have an adopted five-year-old sister from Ethiopia named Kali. He lives near Boston, too, so Bronwyn, Delia, and I can stay with him every other weekend and on Tuesday nights for dinner. ➤

21

It's Sunday, November 21, and today we're in Studio 7 with the company for our first full run-through. That means the entire ballet, from start to finish, with all the dancers. The floor is marked up with tape so it fits the dimensions of the opera house stage.

The artistic staff sits in front of the mirrors, watching and giving the dancers corrections. Even when they're not dancing their parts, the company dancers are sewing their pointe shoe ribbons, stretching, or perfecting their steps in a corner of the studio. All the kids, except for the youngest ones, watch them closely.

We've been at the studio since eleven o'clock this morning, and now it's almost two. Cast B starts at three o'clock and goes until six-thirty. Run-throughs take longer than the actual performance because we have to go over parts that need corrections, work on spacing, and have breaks. All the Claras and Fritzes are required to attend all run-throughs with the company.

We're working on the battle scene. Mr. Nissinen says this is the most dramatic part of the ballet, because it's when Clara discovers how brave she really is. She grows up a little during the battle scene—she's not just a sweet little girl excited about opening presents anymore.

The battle scene starts after all the party guests have gone home and everyone is asleep except Clara. I pretend it's night and that the candle I'm carrying is actually lit. In performance the only light onstage comes from the tree and the candle flame (really a tiny, flickering

bulb). Clara creeps into the living room in her nightgown to check on her nutcracker (*Ah, there you are*, I mime) and falls asleep next to the tree with him in her arms—I'm finally holding the actual nutcracker doll instead of a water bottle.

A great clanging jolts Clara awake. It's the grandfather clock.

What is that thing draped over the top of the clock? she wonders, peering into the gloom. *It's Uncle Drosselmeier! He looks like a bat.*

"Fiona, you have to behave as if you're really scared, how an *actual* girl would act, not like a bun head." Daniel Pelzig, who staged the battle scene, stops the music to instruct me. ("Bun head" is ballet slang for a female dancer, and it's easy to figure out where that comes from.) Mr. Pelzig continues, "Run in looking frightened, as though you've never heard of a single ballet step. Just be a normal girl who finds herself in a strange dream."

Try again. Here goes: twelve clangs of the grandfather clock. Look up with a bewildered expression. Look with fear toward where the clock will be onstage. Run to Columbine (today it's Whitney Jensen) like she's a friend. But then realize that there's something wrong and run toward Harlequin, instead. But something about him isn't right, either. Run downstage, run to stage left. Cry. Here's the Bear. He's gigantic and scary, not soft and fluffy like he was at the party. Plead for help.

"Hold on," says Mr. Nissinen, and claps his hands to stop the run-through again. "Whitney, be sure when you *échappé* that both knees are fully stretched."

We all watch as Whitney Jensen nods her head yes and repeats the step. I don't think I'll ever be able to get that high on my pointes.

"Much better," Mr. Nissinen says. "Let's continue."

The room fills with giant, creepy, crawling Mice. I clutch the nutcracker close in horror and try to fend off their grabbing paws and nibbles. Then, just in time, here's Uncle Drosselmeier. He runs toward me and picks me up as I run

away from the Mice. In performance Dross will climb down a ladder on the back of the clock.

Sabi Varga is Drosselmeier today. He spun me around really fast in the party scene, and I have a feeling from the grin on his face that he's going to do it again now. I can tell by the way he shows us Dross's magic tricks and jokes with us in rehearsal that he remembers just what it was like to be a kid. He's like a big brother—or what I think a big brother would be like, anyway. One day, we had a photographer at rehearsal, and just to be nice Sabi did all kinds of lifts with me. Not many professional dancers would do that.

I remember to pull my legs tightly toward my stomach so when Sabi picks me up this time he can spin me just as fast as before. I think I'm getting the hang of it.

The Mice flee, but the nightmare's not over. I have to imagine that the walls are starting to move, and that the family's Christmas tree is growing so impossibly tall that Clara can no longer see the star on top.

The Mouse King charges into the scene, surrounded by those awful Mice and waving his sword.

"Imagine that there is lots of fog," says Mr. Nissinen. In performance, the stagehands turn the fog machine on full blast, which makes a dramatic puff of smoke around the Mouse King's entrance.

The Mouse King challenges my Nutcracker to a duel. *Please be careful, Nutcracker,* I mime. *The toy soldiers are trying to protect you.*

The Mouse King stabs him!

I have to try not to laugh when getting tickled by the Mice. I remind myself that Clara is *scared.* I'm doing okay, but of course I panic when I throw my (rather stinky) slipper and I miss the Mouse King by a mile. So much for all that practice with my mom.

No! My Nutcracker is hurt, I mime. *He can't stand up. Help, Drosselmeier!*

Then, with a loud bang, the Nutcracker suddenly transforms into a full-grown man. In

performance Drosselmeier swoops his cape over the Nutcracker's head, pulls off his headpiece, and drops it into a laundry basket as he exits the stage. Dross moves so fast that the audience thinks the headpiece just magically vanishes. In rehearsal, we make believe this is happening.

My Nutcracker is a handsome prince! I mime with joy, pretending to touch the crown that Drosselmeier will place on my head. *Am I dreaming?*

Today, Pavel Gurevich is my Prince. He's from Minsk, a city in the Republic of Belarus. Boston Ballet's dancers come from all around the world. I like dancing with Pavel because he partners me like I'm a real ballerina.

THE FIRST TIME I EVER FELT LIKE A REAL
ballerina was when I got to go on pointe, the
summer after fifth grade. All the other girls in
my level, Intermediate 2—that's the sea-green
leotards—had stronger ankles and feet than me,
so they got to go on pointe sooner than I did.

When I finally got my shoes, I was so excited.
I had thought dancing on pointe was going to
be impossible, but it wasn't. It was just difficult.
Even now, whenever I get new pointe shoes my
feet get sore. Sometimes they hurt so much that I
want to cry.

My feet also hurt sometimes because I injured
myself last year. Apparently, I've always had an
extra bone in my left foot, but I only started to
notice it once the extra pressure and stress from
growing quickly caused it to inflame.

All last year I had to go for physical therapy three times a week at Boston Children's
Hospital. My therapist, Mickey, gave me
exercises to help loosen my hips, calves, and
hamstrings. I used Thera-Bands, which are
like giant rubber bands. Mickey also had me
do super-slow *tendus* to strengthen my feet and
ankles. And she showed me how to wrap my
foot to keep me from rolling onto my arches
too much. Now I don't have to go to physical
therapy anymore, but I still wrap my foot and
do my exercises.

Hopefully I will stop growing soon. Growing
hurts.

I use a pad and lamb's wool and sometimes

Band-Aids to cushion my toes in my pointe shoes. I always sew on my own elastic and ribbons. Then I have to wrap and tie the ribbons just right so the knot is on the inside of my ankle.

"Be sure to tuck in the ends. We don't want any straggly bits of ribbon sticking out." How many times do we hear that in pointe class?

Something about my first summer on pointe changed my attitude about ballet. It didn't feel like just a hobby anymore. I was in class every day, from nine in the morning until three or four o'clock in the afternoon. I became serious about getting stronger. And I learned all these new variations, and how to roll up onto pointe without sickling—making sure my toes stretched straight toward the floor instead of turning in. Everywhere I went—the grocery store, the pool, the library—I practiced turning out, stretching, leaping.

"I don't know if it's because I finally got to go on pointe, but now I just can't stop dancing," I told Bronwyn.

"I guess that means you are officially a dancer," she said.

Being officially a dancer meant that I had to quit almost all my other afterschool activities, except for piano, which I still study with my mom. "There are only so many hours in a day," my mom says. I wish we had forty-eight hours or more a day. But if we did, I would probably end up using all that time for ballet, because I love it so much.

Our first dress rehearsal on the real stage is the day before Thanksgiving. The opera house is so much more spacious than Studio 7. It makes me feel small.

We are running the section of the party scene when Drosselmeier waves a sheet over Fritz, making him vanish and then magically reappear in a chair on the other side of the stage. But when Sabi, who is playing Dross in today's dress rehearsal, goes to the chair, Max isn't there. Luckily, Sabi realizes that the little ball curled up on the stage is Max. Sabi quickly lifts Max onto the chair and finishes making Fritz "reappear."

"Okay, let's stop," says Mr. Nissinen, with a smile. He says to Ms. Atkins, "Melanie, would you help Max figure out how to get where he needs to be on time? Everyone else take five minutes, then we'll run the battle scene."

I run to wardrobe and change out of my party dress and into my nightgown. When I come back onstage, I use the few minutes before we begin again to practice my *arabesque sauté*—an *arabesque* with a jump added to it. I'm trying to lift my back leg higher when I'm in the air.

Mr. Nissinen signals for me to come over to him. "Fiona, let's see that *arabesque*." I'm nervous. It's a big deal to get corrections from the artistic director. He says, "Be sure you extend your forward arm fully or the line looks cramped. Misa, would you mind working with Fiona on her arabesque?"

Yikes. I can't believe the Sugar Plum Fairy is coaching me!

"Keep the back of your neck long," Misa says, gently tilting my chin down. "Now the line of your back continues through the top of your head."

AFTER WE FINISH RUNNING THROUGH ACT One, all the kids take a break in the green room. The opera house's green room isn't really green-colored, but that's the traditional name for the room in a theater where the performers wait before going onstage. Some kids are doodling, playing cards, stretching, or writing in their journals. The younger kids' teachers ask them to take notes in rehearsal to help them stay focused and keep track of their corrections.

"I am so tired," I complain to Farin. I grab an apple out of my bag and flop onto my back on the carpet. "My mom woke me up at three a.m. to do my hair!"

"What?" Farin shrieks. "Why?"

"We were both so busy last night that we forgot to set my hair before I went to bed. So we

had to do it in the middle of the night so it would be ready for rehearsal."

For every dress rehearsal and performance, my mom has to curl my hair into long ringlets, the fashion for girls in Germany in the 1800s. The wig master asks girls in the party scene to curl our hair instead of wearing wigs because our own hair moves when we move and falls more naturally around our shoulders when we land from a jump. If we were wearing wigs, the curls would land on *top* of our heads and look strange. So even though they aren't comfortable to sleep with, curlers are worth it.

"I hated wearing the curlers to school today, though. Kids who don't know that I'm a dancer just thought I was a weirdo. And that kid in my math class who always bugs me kept trying to touch them, until Serena grabbed his hand."

I yawn again.

"On the up side," Farin says, "your hair looks great!"

Max comes running over, almost stepping on my leg. He plops onto the rug next to Farin, who's now on her hands and knees arching her back like a cat, and he asks me, "Who's going to play the Nutcracker opening night?"

"I don't know, Max. And I don't want to know."

"Why not? Don't you want to know who you're dancing with?"

Max is nine years old, the same age as Delia. He's usually quiet around girls, but tonight he's asking me almost as many questions as she does. I think it's because he's nervous about the performance.

"It's so, so tempting," I tell him, "but I promised myself that I wouldn't look at the casting list before any of the performances. That way it will be easier for me to make the audience believe that I'm experiencing this magical dream world for the first time. I won't see who is dancing the Nutcracker until his headpiece is taken off and he turns into the Prince."

"What do you talk about when you're in the balloon with the Nutcracker Prince?" Max asks.

"We talk about lots of things. I'll ask questions like, Where did you learn to dance? How old were you when you started? What's your favorite flavor ice cream?"

"Did you hit the Mouse King with your slipper today?" Farin asks. She's not in the battle

scene with me, but she knows how worried I am about it.

"No." I groan.

Two times during past rehearsals I threw my slipper and it bounced off my Nutcracker's sword. I had to go running after it and almost couldn't get it back on before the snow scene. Today I couldn't find my slipper at *all*. I danced the entire rest of the scene with just one shoe.

"I could do without that part," I say to Farin.

"But it's key to the story," Farin points out. "Like, otherwise the Nutcracker might have died and the Mouse King lived and, who knows? The Kingdom of Sweets might have become the Land of Stinky Cheeses or something."

The three of us laugh, and then the stage

manager calls, "Places!" over the loudspeaker, and it's time for me to head back to the stage for Act Two.

THE DRESS REHEARSAL GOES ON FOR nearly eight hours. Counting yesterday's run-through, we've rehearsed more than sixteen hours this week. By the time we get home, it's almost 11 p.m. Bronwyn has to carry a snoring Delia inside from the car. I can hardly keep my eyes open, and my calves feel like they're going to explode.

We head upstairs to our bedroom. We have a bunk bed with a double bottom half. Delia sleeps on top.

"I know I should do my homework now, but I don't want to," I groan.

Bronwyn dumps Delia onto her bunk. "At least neither of us has to miss that much school."

"Yeah, and luckily we have only one matinee during the week." I collapse into bed.

"I'm too tired to think about school—or ballet," says Bronwyn, shoving me over so she can lie down.

"Me too." I crawl under my covers. "Will you wake me when you get up so I can finish my homework before school?" Bronwyn wakes up almost as early as Delia.

But before I hear her answer I'm fast asleep, dreaming about opening night—just two days from now! ➤

Clara doesn't recognize her living room. It feels cold, strange, and frightening. She looks into the darkness and sees Drosselmeier, floating like a ghost on top of the clock. I have no trouble running like a scared girl.

During the entire fight between the Mice and the Soldiers I feel that I'm in a real battle to save my Nutcracker. I throw my slipper at—and hit!—the Mouse King. My wounded Nutcracker lies on the ground.

Then things start to change again. Dross places a crown on Clara's head and waves his cape, and the stage becomes an enchanted winter forest. The Nutcracker has turned into a prince. He takes Clara's hand and they dance together. I remember to *plié* deeply and push off the floor to help the Prince lift me. Otherwise, it's like he's hauling around a sack of potatoes. Not too graceful. And I follow Misa's advice about keeping the back of my neck long when I step into *arabesque*. This small adjustment makes my head and torso feel more connected to my legs and feet.

Now the stage fills with dozens of dancing Snowflakes, running and leaping in big circles, forming patterns with their bodies that look like swirling snow. At the same time "real" snowflakes fall from above, faster and faster, until the ground is carpeted in white. The falling flakes look like frosting, but they're really paper confetti. The stagehands drop about fifty pounds of it onto the stage during the scene.

Jangling bells announce a sleigh pulled by reindeer with glittery white antlers. It carries the

Snow Queen and King, who dance for Clara and her Prince. The Snow King is one of the hardest men's partnering roles in *The Nutcracker*. It has lots of complicated choreography, with big overhead lifts, but James Whiteside makes it look so easy. When James lifts the Snow Queen she seems weightless, like a gust of wind is blowing her off the ground. And I can barely hear a sound when she lands from her jumps. That's something I need to work on.

Would you like to ride in my sleigh? asks the Snow Queen, with an elegant sweep of her arm. *I'm* not too elegant. I almost slip on the snowflakes when I climb into the sleigh—I don't know *why*, since I am basically walking.

There's a loud swooshing sound overhead.

What's this? Clara mimes. *A hot-air balloon?* After a short glide across the stage, Clara and the Nutcracker Prince climb out of the sleigh, dance their way into the balloon's basket, and, with Uncle Drosselmeier flying behind them, soar through the sky to the Kingdom of Sweets. I love feeling the basket wobble a little as it lifts off the stage. It's just a tiny bit scary.

After waving good-bye to the Snow Queen and King, I look into the wings and see the stagehands pulling hard on the rigging that makes the hot-air balloon fly. As we exit the stage, the curtain comes down and the audience applauds. I can hear them rustling as they get out of their seats.

That's how Act One ends. Now we're in the intermission of opening night—twenty minutes until Act Two, just enough time for me to dash to the bathroom, get my makeup refreshed, gulp some water, and climb back into the hot-air balloon basket.

I had been worried about landing the double *tour* and the *soubresaut* (a fast jump keeping my legs tightly together in the air) in the Clara solo. They're some of the most difficult steps, because the heavy dress pulls me back a little, but tonight they went okay. Until my petticoat fell off!

I kept dancing and did a goofy hop so I wouldn't slip on it. Sarah Wroth—she's my governess tonight—acted shocked and mimed for me to come over so we could "leave the party" and get it back on. Oh, and then Max pulled so hard during the tug-of-war that the nutcracker's head rolled practically into the wings. Max is *very* energetic onstage. Other than *those* things, I

think opening night is going well so far. And I'm glad that Sabi is my Drosselmeier tonight. He spun me just fast enough.

And I discovered that John Lam is my Nutcracker. I had no idea until Dross pulled off his headpiece. How does he dance with that huge thing on his head?

"Great aim, Fiona!" Bradley Schlagheck, tonight's Mouse King, congratulates me for smacking him in the head with my slipper as he dashes toward his dressing room.

"Hey, Fiona," says Max, a huge grin on his face, "I bet you didn't notice that I made it to the chair in perfect time for Dross to 'discover' me!"

"I *did* notice, Max," I say, giving him a high five. "You were super fast. Now let me go fix my makeup!"

On my way to the makeup room I run into Bronwyn warming up at the barre and tell her about my petticoat problems.

"Oh, no!" she says. "Sounds like you handled it really well. I'd better make sure my costume is secure before I go on." She carefully examines the elastic band on her Shepherdess hat.

"Look, Bronwyn, here comes Delia," I say, shaking white confetti out of my hair. "Hey, Black Lamb, you look so cute in that costume."

"It's hot and itchy, Fiona. I can't sit down or drink any water or my painted-on nose will get smudged."

"No complaining," I say, positioning Bronwyn's hat at exactly the right slant. "Black Lamb is a

fantastic part, remember? And you are a great jumper."

"Yeah. One time when my cast was practicing, Ms. Markham told me that I was jumping too high, and if I jump that high in the show I will jump higher than the curtain!"

"Places!" commands the stage manager.

"Eeek!" I shout, running to the makeup room, "I have to check my lipstick. Jump high, Delia."

A quick lipstick fix, a sip of water, and I hurry to stage left to climb back into the basket with John Lam. After a short ride, the balloon descends into the Kingdom of Sweets. The snowy forest scene that ended Act One has been replaced by a land filled with dancers dressed in costumes from all around the world.

In Act Two, I get to dance with the Sugar Plum Fairy. I even get to hold her hand. And to top it off, I've got the best seat in the opera house—the wooden throne onstage—and I get to see the amazing company dancers (for free!). I can hear the dancers breathe and give a little verbal support to one another onstage. I've seen the ballet so many times in rehearsal, but I will never get tired of it. Everyone's dancing looks so much bigger in performance.

While I sit on the throne with Drosselmeier, watching the Chinese dance, I have to be sure that I don't do anything distracting or weird, like scratch my chin, which is starting to itch like crazy! Even though I am watching the dancers, I am still performing, so I have to stay in character. The stage lights are hot and so bright that

I can see the faces of the people in the front row of the audience. I'm pretty sure that's Serena and her mom sitting a few rows back.

I look toward the wings and see Bronwyn and Delia getting ready for their entrance with the other Shepherdess and Lambs. Bronwyn is holding her staff and whispering something funny to Delia, who's trying not to laugh.

Here they come! The Shepherdesses are doing their best to keep the Lambs in line. They are so cute, snuggled together in their tiny herd, but the Black Lamb pays no attention and is jumping in front of the throne. I can't help it—I catch Delia's eye and give her a big wink. She grins back and keeps going without missing a beat. I'm so proud of her. Bronwyn looks gentle and calm, like she's in the middle of a beautiful meadow. And her feet look really pretty as she walks on pointe.

Mother Ginger enters—teetering on her stilts—and opens her giant skirt, and out come the little Polichinelles. Dross and I leave our throne to dance with them. As I jump up and start dancing, my legs and feet tingle a little bit from sitting for so long. They were starting to fall asleep. I have to remember for the next show to wiggle my toes while I'm sitting and anticipate the moment I jump off the throne, so my muscles will feel ready to move. I think about Ms. Atkins telling us during a Clara rehearsal that it is just as hard to be still onstage as it is to dance.

The Polis run in a blur around me (*perfect* spacing), the "naughty" Poli does her flips, Drosselmeier and Mother Ginger make the audience laugh during their crazy duet, and Sabi lifts me so high I feel like I'm flying.

All the rehearsals have paid off. I am Clara. ➤

The performance is over! We took our final bows and the curtain came down, but all the dancers in Act Two are still onstage, laughing, hugging, and congratulating one another.

I rush backstage to the dressing room to change into my street clothes so I can meet my mom and my friends in the lobby. I drop my crown in the accessories box and hang up my Clara nightgown.

I pull on my T-shirt and jeans and reach for the tissues and cold cream to remove my makeup. But then I think, no, I want to leave it on for fun. I decide to leave my hair in ringlets, too.

My cheeks are burning because I had to keep smiling throughout the performance, and now I can't stop. At this moment, I know for sure that I want to be a professional ballerina and keep dancing forever.